Published by Ravette Publishing 2003
Copyright © 2003 United Feature Syndicate, Inc.
All rights reserved.
Licensed by PSL
(www.snoopy.com)

PEANUTS is a registered trademark of
United Feature Syndicate, Inc.
Based on the PEANUTS® comic strip
by Charles M. Schulz.

Printed and bound in Great Britain
for Ravette Publishing Limited,
Unit 3, Tristar Centre,
Star Road, Partridge Green,
West Sussex RH13 8RA
by Cox & Wyman Ltd, Reading, Berkshire

ISBN: 1 84161 178 6

MY SECOND
2 in 1 COLLECTION
CONTAINS:

THE FITNESS FANATIC
THE MATCHMAKER

SNOOPY

(features as)

The Fitness Fanatic

Charles M. Schulz

ЯR

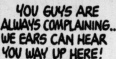

CLOMP!

7-19

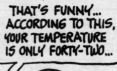

THAT'S FUNNY... ACCORDING TO THIS, YOUR TEMPERATURE IS ONLY FORTY-TWO...

8-5

SOMEBODY MUST HAVE HAD COLD FEET!

SCHULZ

I DON'T UNDERSTAND

HAPPY BIRTHDAY, AMY!

5-5

SUDDENLY I FEEL VERY FAT!

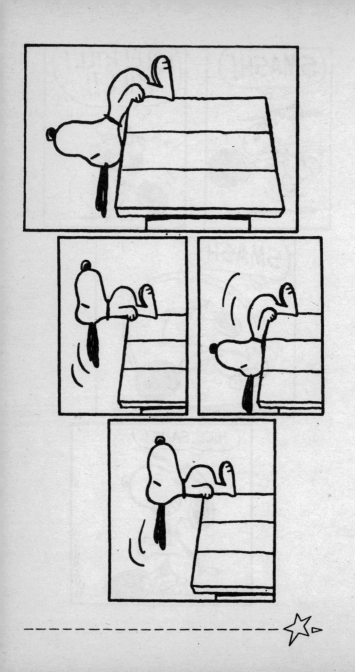

I THINK I'VE DISCOVERED SOMETHING

12-9

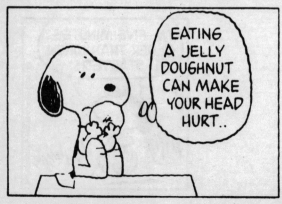

THANK YOU, MA'AM..
WE APPRECIATE IT...

THEY'VE CANCELED
SNOOPY'S KNEE SURGERY

DID THEY SAY WHY?

12-1

DOGS DON'T
HAVE KNEES!

ATTENTION, PLEASE! THIS IS YOUR HEART SPEAKING...

OH, NO, HIM AGAIN.. WE FEET DO ALL THE RUNNING, AND HE DOES THE TALKING!

I APPRECIATE YOUR ALL TURNING OUT TODAY FOR THIS LITTLE RUN...

YOU KNOW WHAT HE'S GOING TO SAY NEXT? "REMEMBER, IF I GO, WE ALL GO!"

REMEMBER, IF I GO, WE ALL GO!

WHAT DID I TELL YOU? ACTUALLY, I THINK THE ARTERIES HAVE HIM WORRIED...

MAKES YOU KIND OF GLAD YOU'RE A FOOT, DOESN'T IT?

MAYBE SO..I HAD AN UNCLE WHO WAS IN THE INFANTRY...HE USED TO SAY,"ALWAYS BE PROUD THAT YOU'RE A FOOT!"

THIS IS YOUR HEART SPEAKING AGAIN... WE'RE NEARING THE END OF OUR RUN..

LET'S ALL BE THANKFUL THAT WE BELONG TO A GOOD OUTFIT

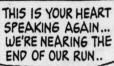

THAT'S RIGHT..

ME!

© 1983 United Feature Syndicate, Inc.

4-17 SCHULZ

5-15

BONK!

THE OTHER DAY I SAW THIS KID AND A DOG PLAYING A GAME..THE KID THREW A STICK AND THE DOG WOULD CHASE IT..

THAT WOULD BE NICE

SNOOPY

features as

The Matchmaker

Charles M. Schulz

ЯR

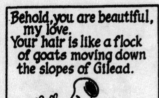

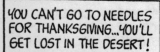

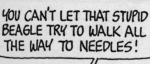

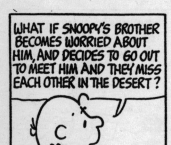

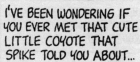

PEANUTS

Napoleon was ready to leave for Moscow.

He kissed his wife, and whispered farewell.

11-30

As he rode off to battle, she shouted, "Don't get blown apart, Bonapart!"

WELL, SHE MIGHT HAVE SAID IT!

© 1977 United Feature Syndicate, Inc.

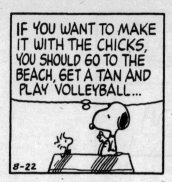

Dear Valentine,

Just a few words to tell you how much I love you.

I have loved you since the first day I saw you.

Whenever that was.

© 1983 United Feature Syndicate, Inc

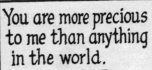

Other PEANUTS titles published by Ravette . . .

Pocket Books	ISBN	Price
Man's Best Friend	1 84161 066 6	£2.99
Master of Disguise	1 84161 161 1	£2.99
Master of the Fairways	1 84161 067 4	£2.99
The Fearless Leader	1 84161 104 2	£2.99
The Great Entertainer	1 84161 160 3	£2.99
The Great Philosopher	1 84161 064 X	£2.99
The Legal Beagle	1 84161 065 8	£2.99
The Master Chef	1 84161 107 7	£2.99
The Music Lover	1 84161 106 9	£2.99
The Sportsman	1 84161 105 0	£2.99
The Tennis Ace	1 84161 162 X	£2.99
The Winter Wonder Dog	1 84161 163 8	£2.99

2-in-1 Collections
new title now available

Book 1	1 84161 177 8	£4.99

Little Books

Charlie Brown – Friendship	1 84161 156 5	£2.50
Charlie Brown – Wisdom	1 84161 099 2	£2.50
Educating Peanuts	1 84161 158 1	£2.50
Lucy – Advice	1 84161 101 8	£2.50
Peanuts – Life	1 84161 157 3	£2.50
Peppermint Patty – Blunders	1 84161 102 6	£2.50
Snoopy – Laughter	1 84161 100 X	£2.50
Snoopy – Style	1 84161 155 7	£2.50

Black & White Landscapes
new titles available

Now, That's Profound, Charlie Brown	1 84161 181 6	£4.99
I Told You So, You Blockhead!	1 84161 182 4	£4.99

Miscellaneous	ISBN	Price
new title now available		
It's A Dog's Life, Snoopy	1 84161 179 4	£9.99
Peanuts Anniversary Treasury	1 84161 021 6	£9.99
Peanuts Treasury	1 84161 043 7	£9.99
You Really Don't Look 50 Charlie Brown	1 84161 020 8	£7.99
Snoopy's Laughter and Learning		
Book 1 – Read with Snoopy	1 84161 016 X	£2.50
Book 2 – Write with Snoopy	1 84161 017 8	£2.50
Book 3 – Count with Snoopy	1 84161 018 6	£2.50
Book 4 – Colour with Snoopy	1 84161 019 4	£2.50

All PEANUTS books are available at your local bookshop or from the publisher at the address below. Just tick the titles required and send the form with your payment to:-

RAVETTE PUBLISHING
Unit 3, Tristar Centre, Star Road, Partridge Green, West Sussex RH13 8RA

Prices and availability are subject to change without notice.

Please enclose a cheque or postal order made payable to **Ravette Publishing** to the value of the cover price of the book and allow the following for UK postage and packing:

60p for the first book + 30p for each additional book
except *You Really Don't Look 50 Charlie Brown* when please add £1.50 per copy,
It's A Dog's Life, Snoopy – please add £2.50 p&p per copy and the two *Treasuries* – please add £3.00 p&p per copy.

Name..

Address ....

....

....

....